Identifying
and
Solving
Problems:
a system approach

Roger Kaufman

UNIVERSITY ASSOCIATES, INC.· 7596 Eads Avenue · La Jolla, California 92037

Cover design and illustrations by Patrick Murgillo

Copyright © 1976 by University Associates, Inc.
ISBN: 0-88390-117-X
Library of Congress Catalog Card Number: 76-5702
Printed in the United States of America

preface

Planning. Doing. These two activities take up most of our days whether our profession requires us to administrate, facilitate, instruct, counsel, or command. Yet far too often we discover that we are involved in these tasks before we have done the essential preliminary spadework. As a result, plans do not work and solutions mysteriously do not solve anything important.

This book provides the basic concepts necessary for successful planning and doing. It is a system approach to identifying and solving problems—a method for maximizing the effectiveness of the decision-making process. The original design was to direct the book only to professional educators, to aid them in producing more learning for the same money, or perhaps the same learning for less money. But it seemed more useful to broaden that concept. Whether we teach, administrate, facilitate, counsel, or command, we are, probably in conjunction with others, making decisions, and all of us could profit from a more systematic process for making them.

The approach will not make anyone an "instant" system planner nor does it give the complete skills necessary for system planning. (For an in-depth discussion of this process, see the author's *Educational System Planning*.) It does not go into the mathematics of input-output analysis, cost effectiveness equations, and sophisticated cybernetic models. The book is intended to be useful to those vast numbers of people in private industry, government service, education, the military and public service who want a method for increasing the coherence of planning and the effectiveness of doing.

Roger Kaufman
Tallahassee, Florida
March, 1976

REFERENCE

Kaufman, R. A. *Educational System Planning*. Englewood Cliffs, N.J.: Prentice-Hall, 1972.

contents

one

understanding means & ends

NEEDS AND WANTS—
AN IMPORTANT DIFFERENCE

Sometimes people want us to buy their solution when they don't know what the problem is. That's what those headlines on the previous page are all about.

People say they NEED luxuries, products, programs, services— all kinds of things they don't have.

But do they believe these things will *fulfill* needs or do they think they *are* needs?

That's more than just an idle question.

We can save

MONEY

TIME

HUMAN RESOURCES

IF we can stop jumping into solutions before we are sure what our problem is.

PICTURE THIS SCENE:

Let's take a closer look at this.

I need a new Cadillac.

Just WHY does our friend want (or desire or require):

A CAR, and/or

A NEW car, and/or

A new CADILLAC car?

And while we're at it, why, particularly, use the word NEED in the statement?

Maybe someone is trying to sell something as a necessity or an imperative when it really isn't!

Maybe a new Cadillac is just one of several alternatives (or options) for meeting the real NEED.

It might help to divide things into two piles:

MEANS and ENDS

And see how that works for our car example.

MEANS	ENDS
Feet Bicycle Scooter Motorcycle Camper truck Economy car	Transportation for work and pleasure
Rolls Royce Mercedes Jaguar Sailing yacht Private plane	Status

It is obvious that most of the time when we use the word "need" we jump right over other possible means (or options) and

LOCK OURSELVES IN . . .
to a solution that might not be the best one to reach the desired "end."

Somehow many of us confuse **MEANS AND ENDS**

when we use the word "need" as a verb—instead of as a noun to describe a gap between two outcomes.

We often jump to premature solutions and get into problems over our heads.

Well, at least he'll avoid the snake.

Look at the confusion everywhere . . .

These opinions are really solutions . . .

in search of a problem.

Let's not confuse **MEANS and ENDS!**

Because that's a lot
of work to go nowhere.

Let's use the *same words* for the same things!

Some definitions:

END: The result, outcome, product . . .

MEANS: The tools, methods, techniques, or process used to achieve an end . . .

NEED: The gap between current results (or ends) and desired results (or ends) . . .

(Notice that NEED is a noun, a thing, *not* a verb; nor is it used in the *sense* of a verb.)

Let's see how these definitions can work for us.

> *The customers (81%) of a bank say "We NEED longer banking hours."*
> *The vice presidents (77%) say "We NEED shorter banking hours."*
> *Tellers (67%) say "We NEED higher pay."*

Look like a conflict? Maybe not—perhaps each group has confused MEANS and ENDS and jumped right to solutions (higher pay, shorter hours, etc.) without defining the NEED as the gap between current results (or ends) and desired results.

Let's see what each group is saying in terms of means and ends.

MEANS	ENDS
Customers: longer sessions	?
Vice Presidents: shorter sessions	?
Tellers: more money	?

No ends or results are stated! We can only *infer* them.

It really makes more sense to decide HOW to do something *after* we know WHAT we are to accomplish.

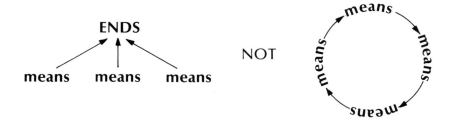

Sound like semantic quibbling? Let's see . . .

Try to sort some of the "hot" issues in contemporary living into means and ends.

	MEANS	ENDS
National health care		
Abortion		
Noncompulsory education		
Malpractice legislation		
Increased government spending		
Preserving the environment		
Speed limits		

Do they turn out to be solutions in search of problems?

If you're not part of the solution, you're part of the problem.

Let's begin by defining your terms.

We can argue almost forever about means

- IF we don't know what we want to accomplish

- IF we don't define the appropriate ends, or outcomes.

> *"A poorly defined problem may have an infinite number of solutions."*

Whoever said that must have worked in my office.

We propose that you can be more

EFFECTIVE

and

EFFICIENT

and

HUMANE

. . . if you will first define the END
before choosing the MEANS.

Shall we try it? Sort the following into Means and Ends.
Which could be ends?

	MEANS	END
Learn aikido	√	
Get a job	?	?
Have a positive self-concept	?	?
Join an encounter group	√	
Teach music	?	?
Move to Bora Bora	?	?
Graduate from college	√	
Survive		√
Love	?	?
Ban adult book stores	√	

Why all those question marks?

You've caught us.

Sometimes something is a MEANS
and sometimes it is also an END.

Some of us want to love so that someone will love us in return.
And we might want to get a job to make money, to buy a car,
to graduate from college.

I'm going to Bora Bora so I don't have to get a job.

Each milestone along the way to an end can be perceived as an end in itself, or as a means to a larger or more distant end.

But what is most important to the success of any venture is to make sure that there is a RECOGNIZED, DEFINED, and JUSTIFIED RESULT we are aiming for—an outcome or *end* to be achieved.

(Actually in the previous list, "survive" is probably the only *basic* outcome or product; the others really relate most to *quality of survival.*)

We must make certain that there is a well-defined distinction and relationship between MEANS and ENDS!

Consider, each time you plan something or do something, what you want to achieve, both:

- NOW, and
- LATER, as a result of this achievement.

But to keep means and ends in perspective, ask yourself, "If I do this, what will be the result?"

If it already is an end, you will know it.

If not, this approach will help keep you focused on results.

Keep asking yourself this question until you have identified the end.

If I buy a new Cadillac...
I will have transportation,
make the neighbors envious,
and get better treatment when
I drive up to a restaurant.

Maybe there's a better and
simpler way to get places.

In problem solving and decision making (whether we are parents, teachers, managers, counselors or just plain persons), results are important.

Why don't we start right now by getting MEANS and ENDS in the correct perspective?

two

where are we going?
and why?

REALISTIC GOAL SETTING

Setting goals, or clearly stating what "end" we want to achieve, is *critical*—if we really want to get from where we are to where we want to be.

The first step in realistic goal setting is to list two dimensions in **MEASURABLE TERMS.**

CURRENT OUTCOMES (or results)	DESIRED OUTCOMES (or results)

If we are now achieving certain results, and we want another result, then we **must** be precise in describing the gap or measurable discrepancy between current and desired outcomes.

For example:

> *45% of our employees have a negative image of the company, and we want to reduce that percentage to no more than 10%.*

Must our outcome statements be measurable?
"Must" is a strong word, but if you really want to make a difference—really to change—then the more precise you can be, the higher your probability of achieving the desired change.

Let's see why

MEASURABILITY

might be so

important.

Look at these two statements of "current results":

I don't like where I work.

My work turns out badly and it takes me longer to do it than it takes my co-workers. I didn't get a promotion and raise when I thought I would. My supervisor always checks on me. And I think George wants my job.

Which statement provides us with more information? Which statement seems most useful?

Which statement allows us to determine:

- WHAT RESULTS WE ARE GETTING NOW

and

- WHAT RESULTS WE WANT?

Sure, the second one is more helpful (and it is also more precise).

The more PRECISE and MEASURABLE we can be, the more chance we have of:

- Making sure we are setting meaningful and appropriate goals;

- Making appropriate choices in getting from where we are to where we want to be.

First, realize that you don't *have* to measure at all—except when you *really* want to make a difference! (If you don't care, or don't want to know, if you have gone from What Is to What Should Be, then don't measure.) However . . .

If you want to change or make a change, the more precisely you measure the more you can know:

- IF YOU ARE ON THE RIGHT TRACK.

- IF YOU HAVE BEEN SUCCESSFUL.

- WHAT SHOULD BE DONE IF YOU ARE NOT SUCCESSFUL.

Did you say **44** long or **34** long?

Measurement and the devices for measurement may be likened
to other tools . . . They are amoral—neither good nor evil . . .

You can use a hammer to bash someone's brains out or you can
use it to build a temple. The user determines whether a tool is
used appropriately.

We don't want to do away with all measurement because some people have misused measurement in the past.
Our job is USING MEASUREMENT to help ourselves and our fellow humans.

. . . and by the way, when we measure, it doesn't have to be in terms of the familiar means and standard deviations—any time we label something we are in fact measuring!

In fact, we know of four scales of measurement:

Nominal

Ordinal

Interval

Ratio

And we suggest that

the more refined the scale of measurement,
the more reliable the measure!

Let's see some possible uses for each.

Nominal-scale measures simply name or label:

If you can *name* something, you ARE measuring! (And if you can't at least name something, like "Love," "Beauty," "Actualization," etc., then you can't really be sure it exists!)

Ordinal-scale measurement involves ranking:

Steak	Chocolate Cake
Lobster	Cherry Pie
Pizza	Hot Dog
Won Ton Soup	Pistachio Ice Cream

We can't say how much more or less each item is, compared to the others. But we can rank them in order by some criterion, such as personal appeal, your taste buds, or your appetite.

With this type of scale, we can say only that one thing is:

- Greater than
- Equal to

    or

- Less than something else.

In everyday language we use ordinal-scale measurements frequently, such as:

Interval-scale measurements are most often associated with science and scientists, but everyone can use them...

They have equal scale distances but an arbitrary zero point. The important thing they tell us is the degree of distance from that arbitrary point.

- Like maps: the equator and the prime meridian at Greenwich are arbitrary zero points.

- Like thermometers: zero degrees, Fahrenheit or Centigrade, is an arbitrary zero point.

- Like clocks: midnight is an arbitrary zero point.

So is getting up to go to work!

We often use interval-scale measurements in planning human change—most of our psychological tests (including ones using those infernal means and standard deviations) are interval-scale measurements.

When we want to plan change, we are best off if we use interval-scale measures or if we use . . .

Ratio-scale measurement. Measures such as feet or pounds are like interval-scale measures, except that the zero point really means "zero." It is a starting place that occurs naturally.

Minus forty pounds?
That's impossible!

Ratio-scale measures are difficult to apply to human behavior, so let's concentrate on

• Nominal • Ordinal • Interval

It's inefficient to use a **less-refined** scale of measurement when we have more precise measures that are valid.

I prefer this car because it has 250 h.p., gets 30 m.p.g., and has a 40,000 mile guarantee.

I like the yellow car better than the green.

. . . Or to try to use a **too-refined** measure when that scale is inappropriate to what we are measuring.

Can you tell me how many fluid ounces of chlorophyll this philodendron contains?

When we set our goals, we are best off if we can state our current results (or outcomes) in INTERVAL-SCALE terms, the most **precise** scale that generally applies to human behavior.

Any statement of desired objectives should do the following things:

- Tell what outcome is to be achieved.

- Tell when the outcome will be achieved.

- Tell what criteria will measure its achievement and under what conditions it will be measured and by whom.

And remember—the more outcome statements that we can make in interval-scale terms, the better will be our

PLANNING

DOING

EVALUATION

REVISION (and Renewal)

Let's look at a possible example for framing an outcome statement that will perform the three functions we mention above . . .

> By the time I am 45, and the children have graduated from college and are out on their own (so that I won't have to contribute money to them), I will be earning $24,000 a year in a job I like, our home will be paid for, my wife and I will enjoy more of life's good things, based upon a greater spendable income than now. We will each own a car. We will dine out more frequently. We will travel abroad for at least two vacations. At home we will buy season tickets to the symphony. I will have put enough money aside to purchase a small income property (under $75,000) for my retirement. My wife and I will be in "good health" as indicated by a licensed physician's physical examination, and we will stay that way with swimming and tennis. We will have at least three couples whom we would rate as good friends (or better) and a larger number of acquaintances. We will visit our children frequently, but not so often that we intrude or interfere, as indicated by their telling us to leave or asking us more than twice in a row not to come.

Notice that this hypothetical What Should Be statement:

- Is measurable.

- Identifies who (or what) will display the desired behaviors and attitudes.

- Lists the criteria for evaluation and the conditions for evaluation.

- Leaves little room for confusion.

It also is PEOPLE-CENTERED!

When you are preparing your objectives (or goals), aside from
making them MEASURABLE, also remember to talk about

ENDS

not

MEANS, or

How-to-do-its.

I think I'll go back and review
Chapter One on Means and Ends.

If you are getting a certain set of results (outcomes) now,
And you want to achieve a different or modified set
you should make two parallel lists . . .
a WHAT IS list and a WHAT SHOULD BE list.

Pick an area of interest to yourself and try it out.

Last season our batting was feeble,
our pitching was soggy,
and our fielding was sloppy.
But THIS year...!

WHAT IS (current results)	**WHAT SHOULD BE** (desired results)
Earning $18,000 a year at age 39	Earn at least $24,000 a year in 6 years
Paying $450 a month principal and interest on house	Pay off mortgage in 6 more years
Own one car	Own two cars
No investment program	Begin by putting aside at least $300 a month for income property and other investments
Sporadic health checks	Regular "check-ups" with physician and certification of good health
Infrequent exercise	Regular exercise

Check your What Is list and your What Should Be list against our criteria for a statement of outcome:

- Do they tell what outcome is to be achieved?

- Do they tell when the outcome will be achieved and what criteria (measures) will be used to determine its achievement?

- Do they tell by whom and what the achievement will be measured?

- Do they avoid ambiguity and confusion?

(If they don't meet all these specifications, go back and revise them.)

You will, probably, have to have more practice writing measurable outcome statements.

Don't get discouraged or lose interest . . .
The trip is worthwhile.

I'm packed
and ready to go!

Anyway, keep at it.

You've probably had quite enough now.

At least

take

a

S-T-R-E-T-C-H !

Want to take other people into consideration?

Most people aren't alone in the world (although we might feel pretty lonely from time to time), and what we do affects others—and vice versa.

So why not take into account these interactions and interrelationships?

When we are selecting goals and objectives, we can involve our partners in NEEDS ASSESSMENT.

Each partner, or group of partners, can (and really should) fill out a What Is and What Should Be statement.

Let's say you are doing some educational planning and you have, at least, the following partners:

Learner or Recipient

Associates: Partners, Co-Workers, Teachers, Administrators

Society: Parents, Clubs, Citizens, etc.

Include a What Is and What Should Be analysis for each group.

	WHAT IS (Results)	**WHAT SHOULD BE** (Results)
Learner		
Associates		
Society		

Remember to make all statements measurable on an interval (or ratio) scale.

Remember, a
NEED
is a gap between

What Is and What Should Be in terms of
OUTCOMES,
or **RESULTS.**

One possible way to keep means and ends separate is to list both means and ends as we have below . . .

What Is (Current Results)	Possible Methods and Means To Get from Is to Should Be	What Should Be (Desired Results)

The means are how you meet or reduce a need... how you get from CURRENT to DESIRED results.

Now the purpose of going through all this is to do a

NEEDS ASSESSMENT

A what?
Can't you say
that in English?

A NEEDS ASSESSMENT is a *formal* analysis that

- Shows and documents the gaps between current outcomes and desired outcomes.

- Arranges the gaps (needs) in priority order.*

- Selects the needs to be resolved.

---

*In doing a Needs Assessment, it is advisable to include an external referent, such as survival and contribution, as well as the perceptions of the partners—sometimes our partners' views are not complete! (See R. A. Kaufman. *Educational System Planning.* Englewood Cliffs, N.J.: Prentice-Hall, 1972.)

When you see the gaps between What Is and What Should Be for you and your partners, you can reconcile any differences (or mismatches) by negotiation, capitulation, manipulation, bribery, etc.

This is the first step in learning to improve decision making. It is essential to planning. It assures us that where we are going is where we should be going, and further, that our partners agree!

It is **PURPOSIVE,**

HUMANE,

and

PRACTICAL.

And I'm beginning to see how it might work.

three

how to get
from here to there
– the bridge to success

If you've done what was suggested previously you have:

- Listed gaps between current outcomes and desired outcomes

- Selected needs—those gaps that have the highest priorities.

  You know WHERE YOU ARE and
  WHERE YOU WANT TO BE.

Now it is time to:

- Perform an analysis to determine all the requirements (specifications) necessary to get from

  HERE ☐ **TO** ⟩ **THERE**

- Identify possible ways and means to get you there in the quickest and easiest manner so that later you can select the *best* ways and means.

- Assure yourself that the "trip" is feasible.

This builds a "bridge" for getting from CURRENT RESULTS to DESIRED RESULTS.

The first thing to do is to use your What Should Be statement as an overall statement of outcome.

This is called the **MISSION OBJECTIVE.**

This MISSION OBJECTIVE (or overall outcome statement) should be written in measurable performance terms:

> By July 23, 1978, the employees of the Ideal Ice Cream Co. will have developed a more positive attitude toward the firm as measured by at least a 50% drop in absenteeism and employee turnover, a 75% reduction in lost orders, and an equal drop in spillage and loading-dock damage. There will also be a substantial (at least 70 percent) increase in the number of positive suggestions from employees to management and a readiness to discuss grievances openly instead of grumbling in small groups, as measured by a questionnaire filled out by employees. On its side, management will recognize problems when they arise and move to solve them at once without letting them build into major, and bitter, issues when union contract negotiations begin at the end of two years, as measured by a reduction in protracted contract disputes. Management will also take the initiative in instituting an employee recreation program on or before this date.

From this Mission Objective, next construct a plan—a **management plan**—of what (regardless of how you get there) "en-route" outcomes are to be achieved to get you from What Is to What Should Be.

We agree.

That will do it.

That would be fine.

I like the sound of that Management Plan.

The management plan[1] is best shown as a series of rectangles that depict the order of, and the relationships between, the en-route outcomes.

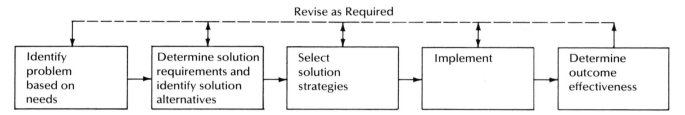

As an example of the most general problem-solving process (model), take a closer look at this one . . .

The first outcome is to:

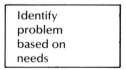

You have accomplished this when you have identified the gap (need) between Current Results and Desired Outcomes.

―――――――
[1]See R. A. Kaufman. *Educational System Planning*. Englewood Cliffs, N.J.: Prentice-Hall, 1972.

The second outcome is to:

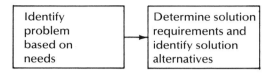

Here *all* of the requirements for getting from What Is to What Should Be are analyzed, and alternative ways and means to meet these requirements are identified.

That's a big job but a sensible way to start getting it done.

From your What Should Be statement, you then draw
successive "mini-management plans" for each function in your
overall plan. This plan, called a **MISSION PROFILE,** looks like this:

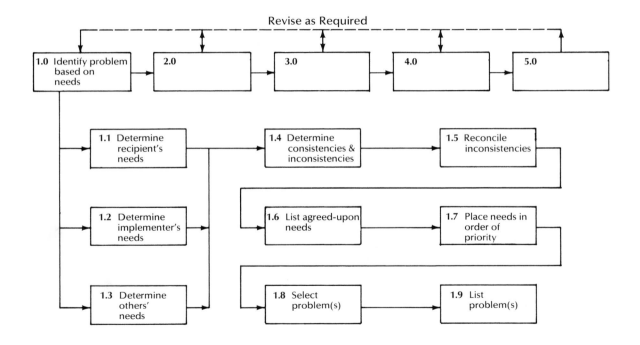

Each phase has a number with a zero after the decimal point: 1.0, 13.0, 14.0, etc.

The process of making a "mini-management plan," or "break-out," is called FUNCTION ANALYSIS—each mini-plan has a number related to its function, such as: 1.1, 1.2, 1.9, 1.1.1, 1.9.1, 1.9.2, etc. The different names and numbers emphasize differences in levels of planning.

What does this FUNCTION ANALYSIS tell you? Put into words, it reads something like this:

In order to identify the problem, based on needs (**1.0**) you:

1.1   Determine the recipient's needs, and

1.2   Determine the implementer's needs, and

1.3   Determine others' needs;

then

1.4   Determine those needs about which there is agreement or disagreement,

...then

1.5 Reconcile the inconsistencies (you might want to negotiate, convince, bully, etc.)

then

1.6 List the needs about which there is agreement,

then

1.7 Place the needs in order of priority,

then

1.8 Select the problem(s) to be worked on (A problem is a "need" selected for resolution), and

then

1.9 List the selected problem(s).

I have to remember that needs are gaps between current results and desired results... products, not processes.

Next, do this break-out (function analysis) for each element in the overall plan (Mission Profile) on as many levels as necessary to define all the requirements and interrelationships . . .

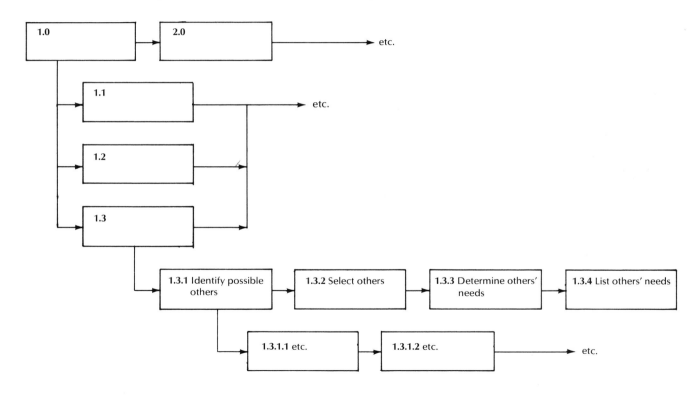

EACH TIME YOU IDENTIFY A FUNCTION

- **List measurable specifications for each one**

and

- **Identify possible ways and means for meeting each specification.**

The identification of possible ways and means is accomplished without selecting "how-to-do-its"—in order to consider

ALTERNATIVES

and

KEEP THE OPTIONS OPEN!

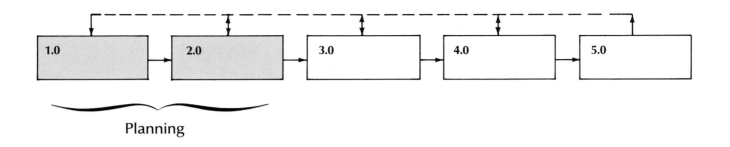

Planning

The First Two Steps (1.0 and **2.0)**
may be considered to be

PLANNING

and the balance is

DOING.

The Third Product

is to select the most *effective* and *efficient* ways and means of meeting the requirements and thus getting from

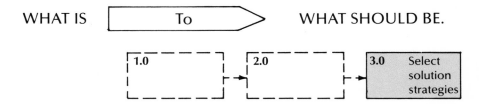

WHAT IS ☐ To ⟩ WHAT SHOULD BE.

The Fourth Product

is to do what you planned   (in **1.0** and **2.0**) with the ways and means you selected (in **3.0**) . . .

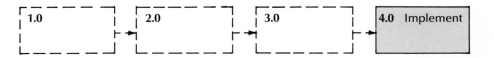

The Fifth Product

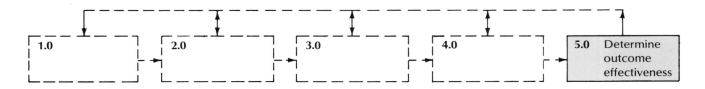

is to determine how well or how poorly the requirements have been met.

You mean I can measure my performance too?

The Sixth Product

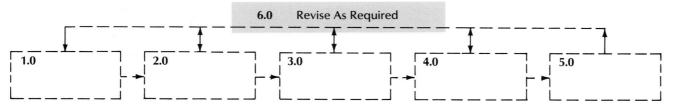

is to make changes any time and any place in your planning and doing process when you are not getting where you want to be—this is a self-correcting process.

This problem-solving process (the jargon term is "a system approach"[1]) is a basic process any time you want to identify and resolve problems.

[1]See R. A. Kaufman. *Educational System Planning*. Englewood Cliffs, N.J.: Prentice-Hall, 1972.

Let's go back to our original MISSION OBJECTIVE:

> *By July 23, 1978, the employees of the Ideal Ice Cream Co. will have developed a more positive attitude toward the firm as measured by at least a 50% drop in absenteeism and employee turnover, a 75% reduction in lost orders, and an equal drop in spillage and loading-dock damage. There will also be a substantial (at least 70 percent) increase in the number of positive suggestions from employees to management and a readiness to discuss grievances openly instead of grumbling in small groups, as measured by a questionnaire filled out by employees. On its side, management will recognize problems when they arise and move to solve them at once without letting them build into major, and bitter, issues when union contract negotiations begin at the end of two years, as measured by a reduction in protracted contract disputes. Management will also take the initiative in instituting an employee recreation program on or before this date.*

With this What Should Be statement, now draw a plan (mission profile) for getting from where you are to the accomplishment you want . . .

Perhaps it would look like this:

By July 23, 1978, etc.

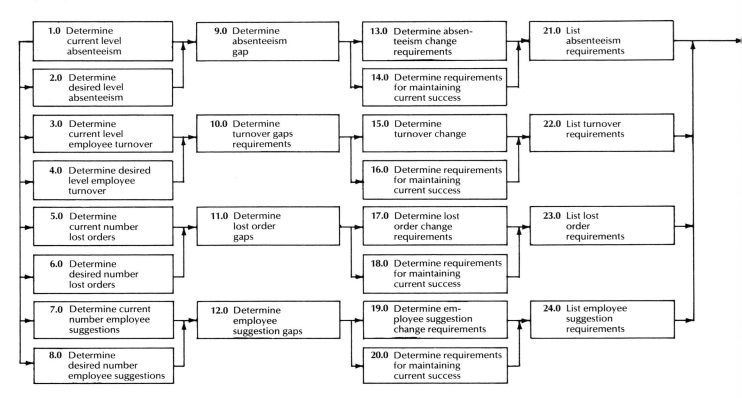

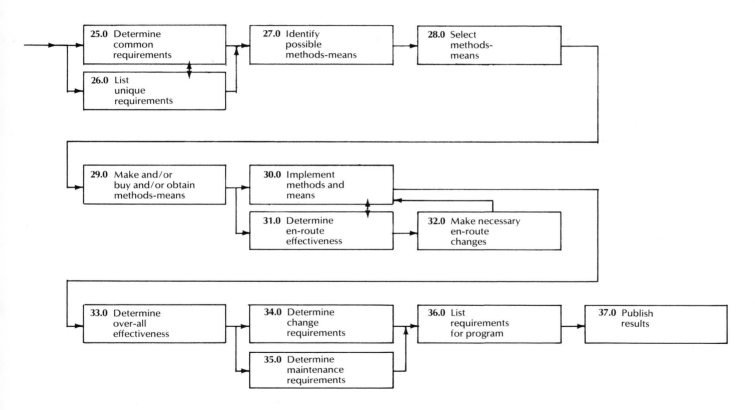

Continue this analysis until you are certain that if you did what you planned you would get from WHAT IS to
WHAT SHOULD BE!

Then . . .

Identify possible ways and means for accomplishing each function. Here is a possible (but hypothetical) methods and means analysis for function number **7.0**:

FUNCTION	POSSIBLE WAYS AND MEANS	ADVANTAGES	DISADVANTAGES
7.0 Determine current number of employee suggestions	**A.** Ask top level supervisors **B.** Ask lower level supervisors **C.** Random sampling of employees in each department **D.** Analyze recent contributions to suggestion boxes	**A.** Fast **B.** Closer contact with workers on the floor **C.** First-hand information **D.** Factual	**A.** Too far removed from workers on the floor **B.** Personal bias enters in **C.** Might exaggerate their contributions **D.** Often impossible to tell how many suggestions come from what number of employees; also, some employees reluctant to write anything

You now have the necessary information for *successful* planning:

- An overall objective (mission objective)

- A plan for getting the objective accomplished (mission profile plus function analysis)

- Alternative ways and means for implementing the plan, including a list of the advantages and disadvantages of each

- The assurance of feasibility (if you hadn't found any ways and means, you would know you couldn't do the job)

You are now ready to go from
PLANNING to DOING!

four

decisions, decisions

Some people like to make decisions—others avoid them.

Either way, DECISIONS GET MADE!

In solving problems with the previous planning and the resulting information, you still have to make decisions—

But now it is

EASIER!

Basically, you can make a wise selection if you

- Know where you are going (mission objective based on needs).

- Know what has to be accomplished to get you from where you are to where you want to be.

- Know the alternative ways and means to get from "here" to "there."

. . . and if you've followed along until now, you have all that information!

Wait a minute! How do I sort out all those alternatives?

Making useful decisions simply involves asking (and answering) two simultaneous questions:

"What do I give?"

and

"What do I get?"

Sounds too easy.
What's the trap?

List your alternative ways and means for doing the job (or getting from where you are to where you want to be) AND select the best ones on the basis of the answer to this question:

What is the highest (or best) payoff for the lowest investment?

(Don't put it off, because
not making a decision…is a DECISION.)

For example:

Alternative	Cost	Result/Benefit
1. Spend vacation visiting our friends the Websters	**1.A.** $75 for travel **1.B.** Sleep on sofa-bed **1.C.** Have to see their tedious friends **1.D.** Have to eat Sally Webster's cooking	**1.A.** Have money left after vacation **1.B.** Get to see old friends **1.C.** Get a partial vacation
2. Go to San Juan	**2.A.** $1355 travel **2.B.** Minimum room & board $150 **2.C.** Nervous when flying **2.D.** Will have to borrow and repay $1,100 **2.E.** Maybe only meet new people I wouldn't want to meet	**2.A.** Vacation will be novel **2.B.** Have good memories **2.C.** Meet new people?
3. Stay home	etc.	etc.

You can see that when you are making decisions about personal goals and objectives, your selection of one option among many may be rather subjective.

When you are in more precise areas like business, science, technology, you can do actual COST/EFFECTIVENESS studies.

Whether you do a formal analysis (usually more effective and efficient) or an informal one, your DECISION is your first affirmative action step.

You have

- defined where you are and where you want to be,

- identified all the steps to be accomplished,

- identified possible optional ways and means to get you there *plus* the advantages and disadvantages of each,

- selected the most effective and efficient how-to-do-its.

In fact

You have decided to **SUCCEED!**

And that's what it's all about!

five

doing what you've planned-well

So you know what you are going to do and how you are going to do it. Your next job is to

Make, buy, or build, or beg, borrow, or steal the
tools for getting the job done

AND

Schedule resources—make sure that what you will be
using will be READY and THERE when you have to use it.

Let's see, nurse. You'd better order one scalpel,
a dozen clamps, surgical needle and thread,
dressings, one cheeseburger, and . . .

Some activities are best carried out when we make out a schedule of:

TIME

EVENTS

and/or

INTERRELATIONSHIPS

Some simple schedules consist of a chart (called a Gantt Chart), such as:

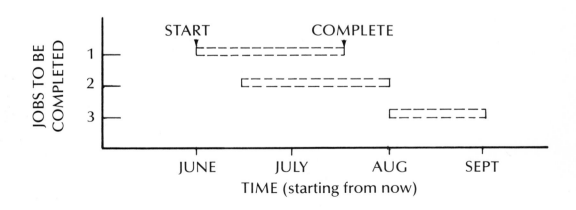

Or a more complex one (called Networks):

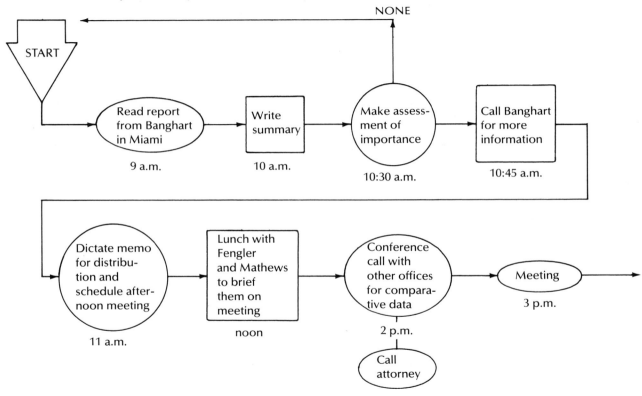

Or a very complex (but usually very useful) one:

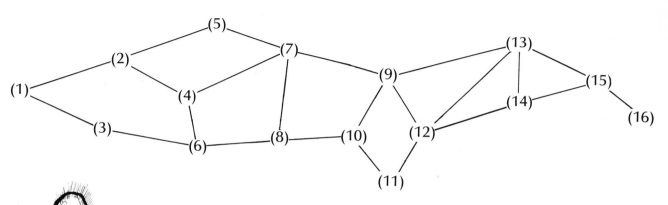

These charts show events, interrelationships between events, and times for each event—and what happens to everything else when some events are early or late.

I've been reading.
This is called PERT—
Program Evaluation Review Technique.

Regardless of how you manage it all, you now are in operation and moving toward SUCCESS, and that requires:

- TIMING

- COMMITMENT

- SENSING AND ADJUSTING

- ORCHESTRATING YOU AND YOUR RESOURCES

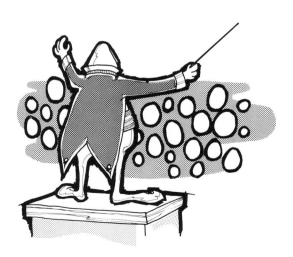

Good management for getting from What Is to What Should
Be is

WORKING SMARTER

NOT

WORKING HARDER

That's good life—management too!

six

finding out how you did

Remember, earlier, how much of a fuss we made about **Measurement** and **Measurability?**

We stated, in measurable terms, where we were going. Now the measurable criteria tell us how to know when we've arrived. We can compare our accomplishment with our objectives.

You mean I can see if I did what I said I was going to do?

So let's compare by using our Mission Objective from page 63:

Objective	Success or Failure
A) 50% drop in absenteeism and employee turnover	A) Success
B) 75% reduction in lost orders	B) Success
C) Increase in employee suggestions	C) Failure
D) Management reducing protracted contract disputes	D) Success

This step allows you to see how well or how poorly you have done what you set out to do. In our hypothetical example we would maintain our performance on objectives A, B, and D and revise our procedures for objective C. We might question the validity of our gap (need) on employee suggestions. Go back to the data collected for functions 7.0, 8.0, 12.0, 19.0, 20.0, 24.0, 25.0, 26.0, 27.0, 28.0, 29.0, 30.0, 31.0, 32.0 (Mission Profile on pages 78 and 79) to assure their correctness and make whatever changes might be necessary.

Evaluation can be your best friend. It can tell:

- Where you were successful
- Where you should make changes—
  where renewal should take place

seven

"if once
you
don't succeed..."

Sad but true, we aren't always successful in doing everything we set out to do—

So your job, both here and throughout, is to

REVISE AS REQUIRED

...whenever and wherever you have not accomplished what you set out to accomplish.

Each time you make a commitment, determine if you are "on target" and if not, where you should revise.

Because all your objectives are written in measurable terms, you can, at any point, see where you are "off target."

At any step of the process, you should go back and re-do whenever you are not getting from What Is to What Should Be.

THIS PROCESS CAN

ACHIEVE

RENEWAL OF THE SYSTEM